Pepperidge Farm Easy Meals for Busy Days was produced by the Global Publishing division of Campbell Soup Company, Campbell Place, Camden, NJ 08103-1799.

Senior Managing Editor:	Pat Teberg
Assistant Editors:	Peg Romano, Ginny Gance, Joanne Fullan
Marketing Managers:	Joe Brennan, Margie Connors, Michael Conway, Ted Kantor, Mike Senackerib, Melanie Thornberry
Public Relations Manager:	Elizabeth Hanlin
Global Consumer Food Center:	Peggy Apice, Kathleen Callan, Jackie Finch, Joanne Fullan, Patricia Ward
Photography:	Peter Walters Photography/Chicago
Photographers:	Peter Walters, Peter Ross
Photo Stylist/Production:	Sally Grimes
Food Stylists:	Lois Hlavac, Moisette McNerney, Gail O'Donnell

Designed and published by Meredith Custom Publishing, 1912 Grand Avenue, Des Moines, IA 50309-3379. Printed in Hong Kong.

Pictured on the front cover: Chicken with Sweet and Sour Stuffing (*page 12*).

Preparation and Cooking Times: Every recipe was developed and tested in Campbell's Global Consumer Food Center by professional home economists. Use "Chill Time," "Cook Time," "Prep Time" and/or "Stand Time" given with each recipe as guides. The preparation times are based on the approximate amount of time required to assemble the recipes *before* baking or cooking. These times include preparation steps, such as chopping; mixing; cooking rice, pasta, vegetables; etc. The fact that some preparation steps can be done simultaneously or during cooking is taken into account. The cook times are based on the minimum amount of time required to cook, bake, grill or broil the food in the recipes.

For sending us dinnerware, flatware, glassware and serving pieces used in recipe photographs, a special thanks to: *Gorham*, Lawrenceville, NJ on pages 9, 19 and 39; *Lenox China and Crystal*, Lawrenceville, NJ on pages 29, 43 and 70-71; *Mikasa*, Secaucus, NJ on page 17; *Mottahedeh*, New York, NY on page 53; *Nikko Ceramics, Inc.*, Wayne, NJ on pages 32-33 and 69; *Reed & Barton Silversmiths*, Taunton, MA on pages 13 and 65; *Taitú*, Dallas, TX on pages 32-33, 58-59 and 67; *The Pfaltzgraff Co.*, York, PA on pages 48-49; *Wedgwood*, Wall, NJ on pages 13, 31, 39, 47 and 65.

Casseroles on the Quick

Delicious one-dish recipes, like *Family-Style Chicken Vegetable Bake*, *Pork Chops with Apple Raisin Stuffing* and *Cheddary Texas Beef Bake* provide a relaxing end to busy days. *Chili Corn Pie* and *Turkey Stuffing Divan* are just two of the family pleasers that can be assembled in minutes. Kick off your shoes while the oven does the rest!

One-Dish Chicken and Stuffing Bake, left (page 6) and Chili Corn Pie, right (page 7).

One-Dish Chicken and Stuffing Bake

  1¼ **cups boiling water**
    4 **tablespoons margarine** *or* **butter, melted***
    4 **cups PEPPERIDGE FARM Herb Seasoned Stuffing**
    4 **to 6 skinless, boneless chicken breast halves (about 1 to 1½ pounds)**
       Paprika
    1 **can (10¾ ounces) CAMPBELL'S condensed Cream of Mushroom Soup**
  ⅓ **cup milk**
    1 **tablespoon chopped fresh parsley** *or* **1 teaspoon dried parsley flakes**

1. Mix water and margarine. Add stuffing. Mix lightly.

2. Spoon stuffing across center of 3-quart shallow baking dish, leaving space on both sides for chicken. Arrange chicken on each side of stuffing. Sprinkle paprika over chicken.

3. Mix soup, milk and parsley. Pour over chicken.

4. Cover and bake at 400°F. for 30 minutes or until chicken is no longer pink. If desired, garnish with *mushrooms* and *fresh parsley*.

MAKES 4 TO 6 SERVINGS • PREP TIME: 10 MINUTES • COOK TIME: 30 MINUTES

* For lower fat stuffing, reduce margarine to 1 tablespoon.

TIP: Substitute 4 cups PEPPERIDGE FARM Cubed Herb Seasoned Stuffing for Herb Seasoned Stuffing.

Chili Corn Pie

    4 **cups PEPPERIDGE FARM Corn Bread Stuffing**
    1 **can (14½ ounces) SWANSON Chicken Broth**
    1 **pound ground beef**
    1 **medium onion, coarsely chopped (about ½ cup)**
    1 **tablespoon chili powder**
  ¼ **teaspoon garlic powder**
    1 **can (8 ounces) whole kernel corn, drained**
    1 **cup shredded Cheddar cheese (4 ounces)**
  ¼ **cup PACE Thick & Chunky Salsa**
      Sour cream

1. Lightly mix stuffing and broth. Let stand 5 minutes or until broth is absorbed. Set aside ½ cup stuffing mixture. Press remaining stuffing mixture into greased 9-inch pie plate to form crust. Bake at 350°F. for 15 minutes.

2. In medium skillet over medium-high heat cook beef, onion, chili powder and garlic powder until beef is browned, stirring to separate meat. Pour off fat. Add corn, cheese, salsa and reserved stuffing mixture. Spoon into crust.

3. Bake 10 minutes more or until hot. Serve with sour cream. If desired, garnish with *cherry tomato* and *jalapeño pepper*.

MAKES 6 SERVINGS • PREP TIME: 10 MINUTES • COOK TIME: 25 MINUTES

Here's a hot tip: Chili powder, a combination of dried chilies, cumin, coriander, cloves, oregano and garlic is available in mild to hot varieties.

Tomato Chicken Supreme

5 cups PEPPERIDGE FARM Cubed Country Style *or*
    Cubed Herb Seasoned Stuffing
2 tablespoons margarine *or* butter, melted
1 cup boiling water
6 skinless, boneless chicken breast halves (about 1½ pounds)
1 can (10¾ ounces) CAMPBELL'S condensed Cream of Chicken Soup
⅓ cup milk
1 medium tomato, cut into 6 slices

1. Crush 1 *cup* stuffing and mix with margarine. Set aside.

2. Lightly mix remaining stuffing and water. Spoon into 3-quart shallow baking dish. Arrange chicken over stuffing.

3. Mix soup and milk. Pour over chicken. Arrange tomato over soup mixture. Sprinkle reserved stuffing mixture over tomato.

4. Bake at 400°F. for 30 minutes or until chicken is no longer pink. If desired, garnish with *fresh parsley.*

MAKES 6 SERVINGS • PREP TIME: 15 MINUTES • COOK TIME: 30 MINUTES

To protect tomatoes from losing their flavor, don't store them in the refrigerator. Instead, keep them unwashed, with the stem end down, on a countertop or windowsill.

Country Chicken Casserole

    1 can (10¾ ounces) CAMPBELL'S condensed Cream of Celery Soup
    1 can (10¾ ounces) CAMPBELL'S condensed Cream of Potato Soup
    1 cup milk
  ¼ teaspoon dried thyme leaves, crushed
  ⅛ teaspoon pepper
    4 cups cooked cut-up vegetables
    2 cups cubed cooked chicken *or* turkey
    4 cups prepared PEPPERIDGE FARM Herb Seasoned Stuffing

1. In 3-quart shallow baking dish mix soups, milk, thyme, pepper, vegetables and chicken. Spoon stuffing over chicken mixture.

2. Bake at 400°F. for 25 minutes or until hot.

MAKES 5 SERVINGS • PREP TIME: 20 MINUTES • COOK TIME: 25 MINUTES

TIP: For 4 cups prepared stuffing, heat 1¼ cups water and 4 tablespoons margarine or butter to a boil. Remove from heat and add 4 cups PEPPERIDGE FARM Herb Seasoned Stuffing. Mix lightly.

Chicken Primavera Bake

    1 can (10¾ ounces) CAMPBELL'S condensed Cream of Chicken Soup
  ¾ cup water
    1 bag (about 16 ounces) frozen seasoned pasta and vegetable combination
    2 cups cubed cooked chicken
    1 cup PEPPERIDGE FARM Herb Seasoned Stuffing
    2 tablespoons margarine *or* butter, melted

1. In 2-quart shallow baking dish mix soup, water, vegetable combination and chicken. Mix stuffing and margarine. Sprinkle over soup mixture.

2. Bake at 400°F. for 35 minutes or until hot.

MAKES 4 SERVINGS • PREP TIME: 10 MINUTES • COOK TIME: 35 MINUTES

Country Chicken Casserole

Turkey Stuffing Divan

    1¼ cups water
     2 tablespoons margarine *or* butter, melted
     4 cups PEPPERIDGE FARM Herb Seasoned Stuffing
     2 cups cooked broccoli cuts
     2 cups cubed cooked turkey *or* chicken
     1 can (10¾ ounces) CAMPBELL'S condensed Cream of Celery Soup
     ½ cup milk
     1 cup shredded Cheddar cheese (4 ounces)

1. Mix water and margarine. Add stuffing. Mix lightly. Spoon into 2-quart shallow baking dish.

2. Arrange broccoli and turkey over stuffing. In small bowl mix soup, milk and *½ cup* cheese. Pour over broccoli and turkey. Sprinkle remaining cheese over soup mixture.

3. Bake at 350°F. for 30 minutes or until hot.

MAKES 6 SERVINGS • PREP TIME: 15 MINUTES • COOK TIME: 30 MINUTES

Chicken with Sweet and Sour Stuffing

     3 tablespoons packed brown sugar
     4 tablespoons margarine *or* butter, melted
     2 tablespoons soy sauce
     1 can (8 ounces) crushed pineapple
     ½ cup water
     1 tablespoon vinegar
     1 stalk celery, sliced (about ½ cup)
     3 cups PEPPERIDGE FARM Corn Bread Stuffing
     4 skinless, boneless chicken breast halves (about 1 pound)

1. Mix *1 tablespoon each* sugar, margarine and soy. Set aside.

2. Mix pineapple, water, vinegar, celery, and remaining sugar, margarine and soy. Add stuffing. Mix lightly. Spoon into greased 2-quart shallow baking dish. Arrange chicken over stuffing. Brush reserved soy mixture over chicken.

3. Bake at 375°F. for 35 minutes or until chicken is no longer pink. If desired, garnish with *fresh parsley* and *carrot*.

MAKES 4 SERVINGS • PREP TIME: 15 MINUTES • COOK TIME: 35 MINUTES

Turkey Stuffing Divan

Home-Style Chicken Pie

        3 cups PEPPERIDGE FARM Herb Seasoned Stuffing
        1 can (10¾ ounces) CAMPBELL'S condensed
             Cream of Chicken & Broccoli Soup
        ½ cup water
        ¼ cup milk
        2 cups cubed cooked chicken
        1 small tomato, chopped (about ½ cup)
        1 tablespoon sliced green onion

1. Reserve ¼ *cup* stuffing.

2. Mix ⅓ *cup* soup and water. Add remaining stuffing. Mix lightly. Spoon into greased 9-inch pie plate.

3. Mix remaining soup, milk, chicken and reserved stuffing. Spoon over stuffing. Bake at 350°F. for 35 minutes or until hot. Top with tomato and onion. Cut into wedges.

MAKES 4 SERVINGS • PREP TIME: 15 MINUTES • COOK TIME: 35 MINUTES

When time is short, two cans (5 ounces each) SWANSON Premium Chunk Chicken, drained, yield the 2 cups chicken needed for this recipe.

Busy Day Chicken and Broccoli

    4½ cups PEPPERIDGE FARM Herb Seasoned Stuffing
     2 tablespoons margarine *or* butter, melted
    ¾ cup water
     1 package (10 ounces) frozen chopped broccoli (2 cups), thawed
     6 skinless, boneless chicken breast halves (about 1½ pounds)
       Paprika
     1 can (10¾ ounces) CAMPBELL'S condensed Broccoli Cheese Soup
    ⅓ cup milk

1. Crush *½ cup* stuffing and mix with *1 tablespoon* margarine. Set aside.

2. Mix water, remaining margarine and broccoli. Add remaining stuffing. Mix lightly. Spoon into 3-quart shallow baking dish. Arrange chicken over stuffing. Sprinkle paprika over chicken.

3. Mix soup and milk. Pour over chicken. Sprinkle reserved stuffing mixture over soup mixture.

4. Bake at 400°F. for 40 minutes or until chicken is no longer pink.

MAKES 6 SERVINGS • PREP TIME: 15 MINUTES • COOK TIME: 40 MINUTES

When shopping for skinless, boneless chicken breasts, the chicken meat should be light in color, not gray or pasty looking. Check the "sell by" label on the package. Most chicken processors specify the last day poultry should be sold.

Busy Day Chicken and Broccoli

Fiesta Chicken and Stuffing

1 can (11⅛ ounces) CAMPBELL'S condensed Fiesta Tomato Soup
1 cup milk
1 can (about 8 ounces) whole kernel corn, drained
2 cups cubed cooked chicken *or* turkey
4 cups PEPPERIDGE FARM Cubed Herb Seasoned *or*
  Cubed Country Style Stuffing
1 cup shredded Cheddar *or* Monterey Jack cheese (4 ounces)

1. Mix soup, milk, corn and chicken. Add stuffing. Mix lightly. Spoon into 2-quart shallow baking dish.

2. Bake at 350°F. for 25 minutes or until hot. Sprinkle with cheese. Bake 5 minutes more or until cheese is melted. If desired, serve with *PACE Thick & Chunky Salsa* and garnish with *fresh cilantro.*

MAKES 6 SERVINGS • PREP TIME: 10 MINUTES • COOK TIME: 30 MINUTES

Two whole uncooked chicken breasts — 1½ pounds with skin and bones or 1 pound without — yield the 2 cups cooked chicken you'll need to prepare this recipe.

Fiesta Chicken and Stuffing

Family-Style Chicken Vegetable Bake

1 can (10¾ ounces) CAMPBELL'S condensed Cream of Mushroom Soup
1 cup milk *or* water
2 cups frozen vegetable combination (broccoli, cauliflower, carrots)
2 cups cubed cooked chicken *or* turkey
4 cups PEPPERIDGE FARM Cubed Herb Seasoned Stuffing
1 cup shredded Swiss *or* Cheddar cheese (4 ounces)

1. In large saucepan mix soup, milk and vegetables. Over medium-high heat, heat to a boil. Remove from heat. Add chicken and stuffing. Mix lightly. Spoon into 2-quart shallow baking dish.

2. Bake at 350°F. for 25 minutes or until hot. Sprinkle with cheese. Bake 5 minutes more or until cheese is melted. If desired, garnish with *tomato* and *fresh herbs*.

MAKES 6 SERVINGS • PREP TIME: 15 MINUTES • COOK TIME: 30 MINUTES

When time is short, two cans (5 ounces each) SWANSON Premium Chunk Chicken, drained, yield the 2 cups chicken needed for this recipe.

Family-Style Chicken Vegetable Bake

Barbecued Chicken and Corn Bread Stuffing

    1 ¼ **cups water**
      2 **tablespoons margarine *or* butter, melted**
     ½ **teaspoon paprika**
      1 **stalk celery, chopped (about ½ cup)**
      2 **green onions, sliced (about ¼ cup)**
      3 **cups PEPPERIDGE FARM Corn Bread Stuffing**
      4 **skinless, boneless chicken breast halves (about 1 pound)**
     ¼ **cup barbecue sauce**

1. Mix water, margarine, paprika, celery and onions. Add stuffing. Mix lightly. Spoon into 2-quart shallow baking dish. Arrange chicken over stuffing. Spoon barbecue sauce over chicken.

2. Bake at 400°F. for 35 minutes or until chicken is no longer pink. Serve with additional *barbecue sauce* if desired.

MAKES 4 SERVINGS • PREP TIME: 15 MINUTES • COOK TIME: 35 MINUTES

Because they are highly perishable, uncooked chicken breasts should be stored in the coldest section of the refrigerator no longer than two days.

Barbecued Chicken and Corn Bread Stuffing

Stuffed Pepper Casserole

2½ cups PEPPERIDGE FARM Herb Seasoned Stuffing
1 tablespoon margarine *or* butter, melted
1 pound ground beef
1 medium onion, chopped (about ½ cup)
1 can (14½ ounces) whole peeled tomatoes, cut up
1 can (8 ounces) whole kernel corn, drained
2 medium green *and/or* red peppers, cut lengthwise into quarters

1. Mix *¼ cup* stuffing and margarine. Set aside.

2. In medium skillet over medium-high heat, cook beef and onion until beef is browned, stirring to separate meat. Pour off fat. Stir in *undrained* tomatoes and corn. Add remaining stuffing. Mix lightly.

3. Arrange peppers in 2-quart casserole. Spoon beef mixture over peppers.

4. Cover and bake at 400°F. for 25 minutes. Sprinkle with reserved stuffing mixture. Bake 5 minutes more or until peppers are tender. If desired, garnish with *yellow tomato* and *fresh chives.*

MAKES 4 SERVINGS • PREP TIME: 15 MINUTES • COOK TIME: 30 MINUTES

When shopping for green peppers, select bright, glossy peppers that are firm and well-shaped. Avoid those with soft spots and gashes. Peppers store well in the refrigerator up to five days.

Stuffed Pepper Casserole

Cheddary Texas Beef Bake

     1½ **pounds ground beef**
      1 **large onion, chopped (about 1 cup)**
      2 **cans (11⅛ ounces *each*) CAMPBELL'S condensed Fiesta Tomato Soup**
      2 **teaspoons ground cumin**
      2 **cups shredded Cheddar cheese (8 ounces)**
      2 **cups water**
     ¼ **cup margarine *or* butter, melted**
      1 **bag (16 ounces) PEPPERIDGE FARM Corn Bread Stuffing**

1. In Dutch oven over medium-high heat cook beef and onion until beef is browned, stirring to separate meat. Pour off fat. Stir in soup, cumin and cheese. Spoon into 3-quart shallow baking dish.

2. Mix water and margarine. Add stuffing. Mix lightly. Spoon over meat mixture.

3. Bake at 350°F. for 30 minutes or until hot. If desired, garnish with *jalapeño pepper*, *celery leaf* and *tomato*.

MAKES 8 SERVINGS • PREP TIME: 15 MINUTES • COOK TIME: 30 MINUTES

You can determine the lean-to-fat ratio of the ground beef you buy by simply checking the label. If labeled "lean" or "extra lean," the meat must have a 25% reduction in fat from the 30% maximum fat content allowed.

Cheddary Texas Beef Bake

Pork Chops with Apple Raisin Stuffing

   1 **cup applesauce**
   ½ **cup water**
   2 **tablespoons margarine** *or* **butter, melted**
   1 **stalk celery, chopped (about ½ cup)**
   2 **tablespoons raisins**
   4 **cups PEPPERIDGE FARM Herb Seasoned Stuffing**
   4 **boneless pork chops, ¾ inch thick (about 1 pound)**
      Paprika *or* **ground cinnamon**

1. Mix applesauce, water, margarine, celery and raisins. Add stuffing. Mix lightly. Spoon into 2-quart shallow baking dish. Arrange chops over stuffing. Sprinkle paprika over chops.

2. Bake at 400°F. for 35 minutes or until chops are no longer pink. If desired, garnish with *apple, fresh chives* and *fresh sage*.

MAKES 4 SERVINGS • PREP TIME: 15 MINUTES • COOK TIME: 35 MINUTES

When buying celery, select a tightly formed bunch with rigid, crisp stalks topped with fresh, hearty-looking leaves. Rinse celery in cold water, shake dry and refrigerate in a plastic bag for up to two weeks.

Pork Chops with Apple Raisin Stuffing

Lemon Herb Fish Bake

    1 cup water*
    4 tablespoons margarine *or* butter
    2 medium carrots, sliced (about 1 cup)
    1 small green pepper, chopped (about ½ cup)
    4 cups PEPPERIDGE FARM Herb Seasoned Stuffing
1½ pounds fresh *or* thawed frozen firm white fish fillets (cod, haddock
        or halibut)
    1 tablespoon lemon juice
    1 tablespoon chopped fresh parsley *or* 1 teaspoon dried parsley flakes

1. In medium saucepan mix water, *2 tablespoons* margarine, carrots and pepper. Over medium-high heat, heat to a boil. Remove from heat. Add stuffing. Mix lightly.

2. Spoon stuffing across center of 3-quart shallow baking dish, leaving space on both sides for fish. Arrange fish on each side of stuffing.

3. Melt remaining margarine and mix with lemon juice and parsley. Spoon over fish.

4. Bake at 400°F. for 15 minutes or until fish flakes easily when tested with a fork.

MAKES 6 SERVINGS • PREP TIME: 15 MINUTES • COOK TIME: 15 MINUTES

* For more moist stuffing increase water by 2 to 4 tablespoons.

*Use your nose
when selecting fresh fish. Fresh fish has a
mild smell, not a "fishy" or ammonia smell.
Make sure the flesh feels springy and elastic
and appears moist and glistening.*

Oriental Chicken and Vegetable Stir-Fry, left (page 34)
and Crunchy Chicken and Gravy, right (page 35).

Sensational Suppers in a Snap

*T*ake the frazzle out of the workweek with *Savory Skillet Chicken and Rice, Easy Salisbury Steak* and other no-fuss favorites. In such dishes as *Easy Baked Pork Chops and Gravy, Herbed Crab Cakes* and *Crunchy Chicken and Gravy,* Pepperidge Farm Stuffing becomes a crispy coating or a flavor enhancer the entire family will enjoy.

Oriental Chicken and Vegetable Stir-Fry

2 tablespoons cornstarch
1 can (14½ ounces) SWANSON Oriental Broth
1 pound skinless, boneless chicken breasts,
   cut into strips
5 cups cut-up vegetables*
4 cups hot cooked rice

1. In bowl mix cornstarch and *1 cup* broth until smooth. Set aside.

2. In medium nonstick skillet over medium-high heat, stir-fry chicken in 2 batches until browned. Set chicken aside.

3. Add remaining broth and vegetables. Heat to a boil. Reduce heat to low. Cover and cook 5 minutes or until vegetables are tender-crisp.

4. Stir cornstarch mixture and add. Cook until mixture boils and thickens, stirring constantly. Return chicken to pan and heat through. Serve over rice. If desired, garnish with *carrot*.

MAKES 4 SERVINGS • PREP TIME: 15 MINUTES • COOK TIME: 25 MINUTES

* Use a combination of broccoli flowerets, green onions cut into 1-inch pieces, sliced celery and sliced carrot.

When it comes to selecting fresh broccoli, the subject is closed! Look for heads with compact clusters of tightly closed flowerets that are dark green, not yellowish. Avoid heads with broad, woody stems.

Crunchy Chicken and Gravy

    1 cup PEPPERIDGE FARM Herb Seasoned Stuffing, crushed
    2 tablespoons grated Parmesan cheese
    4 skinless, boneless chicken breast halves (about 1 pound)
    1 egg, beaten
    2 tablespoons margarine *or* butter, melted
    1 jar (12 ounces) PEPPERIDGE FARM Golden Chicken Gravy

1. Mix stuffing and cheese on plate.

2. Dip chicken into egg. Coat with stuffing mixture.

3. Place chicken on baking sheet. Drizzle with margarine. Bake at 400°F. for 20 minutes or until chicken is no longer pink.

4. In small saucepan over medium heat, heat gravy. Serve with chicken.

MAKES 4 SERVINGS • PREP TIME: 10 MINUTES • COOK TIME: 20 MINUTES

Chicken Dijon

    2 tablespoons margarine *or* butter
    4 skinless, boneless chicken breast halves (about 1 pound)
    1 medium onion, chopped (about ½ cup)
    1 can (10¾ ounces) CAMPBELL'S condensed Cream of Mushroom Soup
¼ cup apple juice *or* milk
    1 tablespoon Dijon-style mustard
    1 tablespoon chopped fresh parsley
    4 cups hot cooked medium egg noodles

1. In medium skillet over medium-high heat, heat *half* the margarine. Add chicken and cook 10 minutes or until browned. Set chicken aside.

2. Reduce heat to medium. Add remaining margarine. Add onion and cook until tender.

3. Add soup, apple juice, mustard and parsley. Heat to a boil. Return chicken to pan. Reduce heat to low. Cover and cook 5 minutes or until chicken is no longer pink. Serve with noodles.

MAKES 4 SERVINGS • PREP TIME: 10 MINUTES • COOK TIME: 25 MINUTES

Savory Skillet Chicken and Rice

      1 **tablespoon margarine** *or* **butter**
      1 **pound skinless, boneless chicken breasts, cut up**
      1 **can (10¾ ounces) CAMPBELL'S condensed Cream of Mushroom Soup**
      1 **cup milk**
      1 **tablespoon onion flakes**
      ¼ **teaspoon dried thyme leaves, crushed**
      ⅛ **teaspoon pepper**
      2 **cups fresh** *or* **frozen cut green beans**
      2 **cups uncooked instant rice**

1. In medium skillet over medium-high heat, heat margarine. Add chicken and cook until browned, stirring often. Set chicken aside.

2. Add soup, milk, onion flakes, thyme, pepper and beans. Heat to a boil. Return chicken to pan. Reduce heat to low. Cover and cook 5 minutes or until chicken is no longer pink.

3. Stir in rice. Cover and remove from heat. Let stand 5 minutes. Fluff with fork. If desired, garnish with *tomato*.

MAKES 4 SERVINGS • PREP TIME: 10 MINUTES • COOK TIME: 20 MINUTES • STAND TIME: 5 MINUTES

Hot Turkey Sandwiches

      1 **jar (12 ounces) PEPPERIDGE FARM Seasoned Turkey Gravy**
      1 **tablespoon prepared mustard (optional)**
     12 **slices cooked turkey (about ¾ pound)**
      4 **long sandwich rolls, split** *or* **8 slices bread**

1. In medium skillet mix gravy and mustard. Over medium heat, heat to a boil.

2. Add turkey. Reduce heat to low and heat through. Serve over rolls.

MAKES 4 SANDWICHES • PREP TIME: 5 MINUTES • COOK TIME: 10 MINUTES

Savory Skillet Chicken and Rice

Easy Chicken and Rotisserie Gravy

    4 **skinless, boneless chicken breast halves (about 1 pound)**
       Paprika (optional)
    1 **tablespoon vegetable oil**
    1 **jar (12 ounces) PEPPERIDGE FARM Rotisserie Chicken Gravy**
    4 **cups hot mashed potatoes *or* prepared**
          PEPPERIDGE FARM Herb Seasoned Stuffing

1. Sprinkle both sides of chicken with paprika.

2. In medium skillet over medium-high heat, heat oil. Add chicken and cook 10 minutes or until browned. Set chicken aside.

3. Add gravy. Heat to a boil. Return chicken to pan. Reduce heat to low. Cover and cook 5 minutes or until chicken is no longer pink. Serve with potatoes.

MAKES 4 SERVINGS • PREP TIME: 5 MINUTES • COOK TIME: 20 MINUTES

TIP: For 4 cups prepared stuffing, heat 1¼ cups water and 4 tablespoons margarine or butter to a boil. Remove from heat and add 4 cups PEPPERIDGE FARM Herb Seasoned Stuffing. Mix lightly.

Golden Chicken with Stuffing

    1 **tablespoon vegetable oil**
    1 **pound skinless, boneless chicken breasts, cut up**
    1 **jar (12 ounces) PEPPERIDGE FARM Golden Chicken Gravy**
    1 **teaspoon lemon juice**
    ¼ **teaspoon dried thyme leaves, crushed**
    4 **cups hot prepared PEPPERIDGE FARM Herb Seasoned Stuffing**
          ***or* mashed potatoes**

1. In medium skillet over medium-high heat, heat oil. Add chicken and cook until browned, stirring often. Set chicken aside.

2. Add gravy, lemon juice and thyme. Heat to a boil. Return chicken to pan. Reduce heat to low. Cover and cook 5 minutes or until chicken is no longer pink. Serve over stuffing.

MAKES 4 SERVINGS • PREP TIME: 10 MINUTES • COOK TIME: 20 MINUTES

Easy Chicken and Rotisserie Gravy

Skillet Sausage and Stuffing

    1 pound sweet *or* hot Italian pork sausage, cut into 1-inch pieces
1¼ cups water*
    1 medium onion, cut into wedges
    1 small green *and/or* red pepper, cut into 2-inch-long strips (about 1 cup)
    4 cups PEPPERIDGE FARM Herb Seasoned Stuffing

1. In medium skillet over medium-high heat, cook sausage until browned, stirring often. Pour off fat.

2. Add water, onion and pepper. Heat to a boil. Reduce heat to low. Cover and cook 5 minutes or until sausage is no longer pink. Remove from heat.

3. Add stuffing. Mix lightly. Cover and let stand 5 minutes or until stuffing is softened.

MAKES 4 SERVINGS • PREP TIME: 10 MINUTES • COOK TIME: 20 MINUTES • STAND TIME: 5 MINUTES

* For more moist stuffing, increase water by 2 to 4 tablespoons.

Easy Baked Pork Chops and Gravy

    4 boneless pork chops, ¾ inch thick (about 1 pound)
    2 tablespoons all-purpose flour
    1 egg, beaten
    1 cup PEPPERIDGE FARM Herb Seasoned Stuffing, crushed
    1 jar (12 ounces) PEPPERIDGE FARM Roasted Onion and Garlic Gravy

1. Lightly coat chops with flour. Dip into egg. Coat with stuffing.

2. Place chops on baking sheet. Bake at 400°F. for 20 minutes or until chops are no longer pink.

3. In small saucepan over medium heat, heat gravy. Serve with chops.

MAKES 4 SERVINGS • PREP TIME: 10 MINUTES • COOK TIME: 20 MINUTES

Skillet Sausage and Stuffing

Herb Seasoned Meat Loaves

       2 **pounds ground beef**
    1½ **cups PEPPERIDGE FARM Herb Seasoned Stuffing**
       2 **eggs, beaten**
       1 **medium onion, finely chopped (about ½ cup)**
      ½ **cup ketchup**
       1 **tablespoon Worcestershire sauce (optional)**
       1 **jar (12 ounces) PEPPERIDGE FARM Hearty Beef Gravy**

1. Mix beef, stuffing, eggs, onion, ketchup and Worcestershire *thoroughly*. In large baking pan shape *firmly* into two 6½- by 4-inch loaves.

2. Bake at 350°F. for 1 hour or until meat loaves are done (160°F.).

3. In small saucepan over medium heat, heat gravy. Serve with meat loaves. If desired, garnish with *green onion*.

MAKES 8 SERVINGS • PREP TIME: 15 MINUTES • COOK TIME: 1 HOUR

Easy Salisbury Steak

       1 **pound ground beef**
      ⅓ **cup PEPPERIDGE FARM Herb Seasoned Stuffing, crushed**
       2 **tablespoons finely chopped onion**
       1 **egg, beaten**
       1 **tablespoon vegetable oil**
       1 **jar (12 ounces) PEPPERIDGE FARM Hearty Beef Gravy**
       1 **jar (about 4½ ounces) sliced mushrooms, drained (optional)**
       4 **cups hot mashed potatoes**

1. Mix beef, stuffing, onion and egg *thoroughly*. Shape *firmly* into 4 patties, ½ inch thick.

2. In medium skillet over medium-high heat, heat oil. Add patties and cook 10 minutes or until browned. Set patties aside. Pour off fat.

3. Add gravy and mushrooms. Heat to a boil. Return patties to pan. Reduce heat to low. Cover and cook 5 minutes or until patties are no longer pink (160°F.). Serve with potatoes.

MAKES 4 SERVINGS • PREP TIME: 10 MINUTES • COOK TIME: 15 MINUTES

Sesame Beef and Peppers

1 pound boneless beef sirloin *or* top round steak, ¾ inch thick
2 tablespoons vegetable oil
1 large green *and/or* red pepper, cut into 2-inch-long strips (about 2 cups)
1 large onion, sliced (about 1 cup)
¼ teaspoon garlic powder
1 jar (12 ounces) PEPPERIDGE FARM Hearty Beef Gravy
1 tablespoon soy sauce
1 tablespoon sesame oil (optional)
4 cups hot cooked rice

1. Slice beef into very thin strips. In skillet over medium-high heat, heat *half* the vegetable oil. Add beef and cook in 2 batches until browned, stirring often. Set beef aside.

2. Reduce heat to medium. Add remaining vegetable oil. Add pepper, onion and garlic powder and cook until tender-crisp.

3. Add gravy, soy and sesame oil. Heat to a boil. Return beef to pan and heat through. Serve over rice.

MAKES 4 SERVINGS • PREP TIME: 15 MINUTES • COOK TIME: 25 MINUTES

Beefy Vegetable Skillet

1 pound ground beef
1 medium onion, chopped (about ½ cup)
2 medium zucchini, quartered lengthwise and sliced
1 can (about 14½ ounces) stewed tomatoes
2 cups PEPPERIDGE FARM Cubed Herb Seasoned Stuffing
2 tablespoons grated Parmesan cheese

1. In medium skillet over medium-high heat, cook beef and onion until beef is browned, stirring to separate meat. Pour off fat.

2. Add zucchini and tomatoes. Heat to a boil. Reduce heat to low. Cover and cook 5 minutes or until zucchini is tender, stirring occasionally. Remove from heat.

3. Add stuffing and cheese. Mix lightly. Cover and let stand 5 minutes.

MAKES 4 SERVINGS • PREP TIME: 10 MINUTES • COOK TIME: 15 MINUTES • STAND TIME: 5 MINUTES

Sesame Beef and Peppers

Golden Baked Catfish

  1 **cup PEPPERIDGE FARM Corn Bread Stuffing, crushed**
  ½ **teaspoon paprika**
  1 **pound catfish fillets**
  1 **egg, beaten**
  2 **tablespoons margarine** *or* **butter, melted (optional)**
     Refrigerated MARIE'S Chunky Blue Cheese *or* **Creamy Ranch**
       Dressing and Dip

1. Mix stuffing and paprika on plate.

2. Dip fish into egg. Coat with stuffing mixture.

3. Place fish on baking sheet. Drizzle with margarine. Bake at 400°F. for 20 minutes or until fish flakes easily when tested with a fork. Serve with dressing.

MAKES 4 SERVINGS • PREP TIME: 10 MINUTES • COOK TIME: 20 MINUTES

Herbed Crab Cakes

  1½ **cups PEPPERIDGE FARM Herb Seasoned Stuffing**
   2 **eggs, beaten**
  ⅓ **cup mayonnaise**
   2 **teaspoons Dijon-style mustard**
   1 **teaspoon Worcestershire sauce**
   1 **tablespoon chopped fresh parsley** *or* **1 teaspoon dried parsley flakes**
   1 **can (16 ounces) refrigerated pasteurized crabmeat**
   2 **tablespoons margarine** *or* **butter**
     Lemon wedges

1. Finely crush *½ cup* stuffing. Set aside.

2. *Lightly* mix remaining stuffing, eggs, mayonnaise, mustard, Worcestershire, parsley and crabmeat. Shape *firmly* into 6 patties, ½ inch thick. Coat with reserved stuffing.

3. In medium skillet over medium heat, heat margarine. Cook patties in 2 batches 5 minutes or until hot.* Serve with lemon wedges.

MAKES 6 SERVINGS • PREP TIME: 15 MINUTES • COOK TIME: 10 MINUTES

* Use additional margarine if necessary.

Holidays without the Hurry

From a Thanksgiving *Turkey with Cranberry Nut Stuffing* to *Ham and Asparagus Strata* for Easter brunch, Pepperidge Farm brings old-fashioned flavor to all your holidays. *Cornish Hens with Pecan Stuffing* and an easy-to-fix *Shrimp Stuffing au Gratin* make holiday meals special, for the cook *and* the guests.

Sunday Best Roast Chicken, left (page 50) and Shrimp Stuffing au Gratin, right (page 51).

Sunday Best Roast Chicken

¼ cup margarine *or* butter
1 stalk celery, sliced (about ½ cup)
1 medium onion, chopped (about ½ cup)
1¼ cups water
1 medium carrot, shredded (about ½ cup) (optional)
4 cups PEPPERIDGE FARM Herb Seasoned Stuffing
5- to 7-pound roasting chicken
Vegetable oil
1 jar (12 ounces) PEPPERIDGE FARM Golden Chicken Gravy

1. In large saucepan over medium heat, heat margarine. Add celery and onion and cook until tender. Stir in water and carrot. Add stuffing. Mix lightly.

2. Remove package of giblets and neck from chicken cavity. Rinse chicken with cold water and pat dry. Spoon stuffing lightly into neck and body cavities.* Fold loose skin over stuffing. Tie ends of drumsticks together. Place chicken, breast side up, on rack in shallow roasting pan. Brush with oil. Insert meat thermometer into thickest part of thigh next to the body, *not touching bone.*

3. Roast at 325°F. for 2½ to 3 hours or until thermometer reads 180°F. and drumstick moves easily, basting occasionally with pan drippings. Begin checking doneness after 2 hours roasting time. Allow chicken to stand 10 minutes before slicing.

4. In small saucepan over medium heat, heat gravy. Serve with chicken.

MAKES 6 TO 8 SERVINGS • PREP TIME: 30 MINUTES • COOK TIME: 2½ TO 3 HOURS • STAND TIME: 10 MINUTES

* Bake any remaining stuffing in covered casserole with chicken 30 minutes or until hot.

Make Sundays Special Menu

Fresh Fruit Compote
Sunday Best Roast Chicken
Golden Pea and Onion Bake (p. 74)
Quick Seasoned Potatoes (p. 62)
Salad
Ice Cream and Assorted Pepperidge Farm Cookies

Shrimp Stuffing au Gratin

4½ cups PEPPERIDGE FARM Herb Seasoned Stuffing
3 tablespoons margarine *or* butter, melted
1¼ cups water
2 cups cooked broccoli flowerets
2 cups cooked medium shrimp
1 can (10¾ ounces) CAMPBELL'S condensed Cream of Mushroom Soup
½ cup milk
2 tablespoons diced pimiento (optional)
1 cup shredded Swiss cheese (4 ounces)

1. Crush *½ cup* stuffing and mix with *1 tablespoon* margarine. Set aside.

2. Mix water and remaining margarine. Add remaining stuffing. Mix lightly. Spoon into 2-quart shallow baking dish.

3. Arrange broccoli and shrimp over stuffing. In small bowl mix soup, milk, pimiento and cheese. Pour over broccoli and shrimp. Sprinkle reserved stuffing mixture over soup mixture.

4. Bake at 350°F. for 30 minutes or until hot. If desired, garnish with *fresh chives*.

MAKES 6 SERVINGS • PREP TIME: 15 MINUTES • COOK TIME: 30 MINUTES

TIP: For 2 cups cooked medium shrimp, in medium saucepan over medium heat, in 4 cups boiling water, cook 1 pound medium shrimp, 1 to 3 minutes or until shrimp turn pink. Rinse immediately under cold water. Shell and devein.

Ring in the New Year Celebration Menu

Savory Stuffed Mushrooms (p. 85)
Shrimp Stuffing au Gratin
Rice
Caesar Salad
Assorted Rolls
Chocolate Mousse Parfaits

Turkey with Cranberry Nut Stuffing

¼ **cup margarine** *or* **butter**
2 **stalks celery, sliced (about 1 cup)**
1 **large onion, chopped (about 1 cup)**
1 **can (14½ ounces) SWANSON Chicken Broth**
½ **cup cranberries**
½ **cup chopped walnuts**
1 **bag (14 ounces) PEPPERIDGE FARM Cubed Country Style** *or*
   Cubed Herb Seasoned Stuffing
12- **to 14-pound turkey**
   Vegetable oil
2 **jars (12 ounces** *each***) PEPPERIDGE FARM Seasoned Turkey Gravy**

1. In large saucepan over medium heat, heat margarine. Add celery and onion and cook until tender. Add broth. Heat to a boil. Remove from heat. Stir in cranberries and walnuts. Add stuffing. Mix lightly.

2. Remove package of giblets and neck from turkey cavity. Rinse turkey with cold water and pat dry. Spoon stuffing lightly into neck and body cavities *(fig. A)*.* Fold loose skin over stuffing. Tie ends of drumsticks together. Place turkey, breast side up, on rack in shallow roasting pan. Brush with oil. Insert meat thermometer deep into thickest part of thigh next to body, *not touching bone (fig. B)*.

3. Roast at 325°F. for 4½ to 5 hours or until thermometer reads 180°F. and drumstick moves easily, basting occasionally with pan drippings. Begin checking doneness after 4 hours roasting time. Allow turkey to stand 10 minutes before slicing.

4. In small saucepan over medium heat, heat gravy. Serve with turkey.

MAKES 12 TO 16 SERVINGS • PREP TIME: 30 MINUTES • COOK TIME: 4½ TO 5 HOURS • STAND TIME: 10 MINUTES

* Bake any remaining stuffing in covered casserole with turkey 30 minutes or until hot.

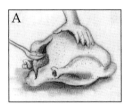

fig. A–Lightly spoon stuffing into body cavity. *Do not pack.* As stuffing bakes it absorbs juices and expands.

fig. B–Insert meat thermometer deep into thickest part of thigh next to body, *not touching bone.*

Cornish Hens with Pecan Stuffing

    1 **can (14½ ounces) SWANSON Chicken Broth**
    4 **green onions, sliced (about ½ cup)**
    ½ **cup chopped pecans**
    ½ **cup golden raisins**
    4 **cups PEPPERIDGE FARM Herb Seasoned Stuffing**
    3 **Cornish game hens (about 1½ pounds *each*), split in half**
    ½ **cup peach preserves**
    1 **tablespoon Dijon-style mustard**

1. Mix broth, onions, pecans and raisins. Add stuffing. Mix lightly. Spoon across center of greased 3-quart shallow baking dish, leaving space on both sides for hens. Arrange hens on each side of stuffing.

2. Mix preserves and mustard. Spoon over hens.

3. Bake at 350°F. for 1 to 1¼ hours or until hens are no longer pink.* Stir glaze and spoon over hens before serving. If desired, garnish with *green onion*.

MAKES 6 SERVINGS • PREP TIME: 15 MINUTES • COOK TIME: 1 TO 1¼ HOURS

* When stuffing is golden brown, cover loosely with foil.

Festive Holiday Dinner Menu
Stuffed Clams (p. 88)
Cornish Hens with Pecan Stuffing
Glazed Carrots
Spinach and Orange Salad
Relish Tray
Dinner Rolls
Cheesecake with Assorted Toppings

Cornish Hens with Pecan Stuffing

Ham and Asparagus Strata

    4 **cups PEPPERIDGE FARM Cubed Country Style Stuffing**
    2 **cups shredded Swiss cheese (8 ounces)**
  1½ **cups cooked cut asparagus**
  1½ **cups cubed cooked ham**
    1 **can (10¾ ounces) CAMPBELL'S condensed Cream of Asparagus Soup**
    2 **cups milk**
    5 **eggs, beaten**
    1 **tablespoon Dijon-style mustard**

1. Mix stuffing, cheese, asparagus and ham. Spoon into greased 3-quart shallow baking dish.

2. Mix soup, milk, eggs and mustard. Pour over stuffing mixture.

3. Bake at 350°F. for 45 minutes or until knife inserted near center comes out clean.
Let stand 5 minutes. If desired, garnish with *fresh oregano.*

MAKES 8 SERVINGS • PREP TIME: 15 MINUTES • COOK TIME: 45 MINUTES • STAND TIME: 5 MINUTES

TIP: For 1½ cups cooked cut asparagus use ¾ pound fresh asparagus, trimmed and cut into 1-inch pieces, *or* 1 package (about 10 ounces) frozen asparagus spears, thawed, drained and cut into 1-inch pieces.

Easy-on-You Spring Brunch

Tomato and Orange Juices
Ham and Asparagus Strata
Fresh Melon and Berries
Croissants and Jam
Cinnamon Bread Pudding (p. 80)
Coffee and Tea

Low-Fat Favorites with Flair

*H*ere's the skinny on low-fat cooking: Use Swanson Broth instead of butter or milk. *Harvest Fruit Stuffing* and *Quick Seasoned Potatoes* retain all their rich full flavor. *Lemon Honey Chicken and Stuffing, Beef and Broccoli* and a host of other entrées make it easy to keep your diet on track. Low-fat meals never tasted this good!

Lemon Honey Chicken and Stuffing, left (page 60)
and Beef and Broccoli, right (page 61).

Lemon Honey Chicken and Stuffing

1 can (14½ ounces) SWANSON Chicken Broth
2 medium carrots, shredded (about 1 cup)
4 cups PEPPERIDGE FARM Herb Seasoned Stuffing
6 chicken breast halves (about 3 pounds), skinned
2 tablespoons honey
2 tablespoons lemon juice
1 tablespoon chopped fresh parsley *or* 1 teaspoon dried parsley flakes
3 lemon slices

1. In large saucepan mix broth and carrots. Over medium-high heat, heat to a boil. Remove from heat. Add stuffing. Mix lightly.

2. Spoon into greased 3-quart shallow baking dish. Arrange chicken over stuffing.

3. Bake at 375°F. for 50 minutes.

4. Mix honey, lemon juice and parsley. Brush over chicken. Cut lemon slices in half and place over chicken. Bake 10 minutes more or until chicken is no longer pink. Remove chicken. Stir stuffing.

MAKES 6 SERVINGS • PREP TIME: 15 MINUTES • COOK TIME: 1 HOUR

✦ *5 grams total fat per serving*

Keep it lean—when using chicken or turkey, remove the skin. For even less fat, choose light meat more often than dark meat.

Beef and Broccoli

1 pound boneless top round steak, ¾ inch thick
2 tablespoons cornstarch
1 can (14½ ounces) SWANSON Beef Broth
1 tablespoon packed brown sugar
1 tablespoon soy sauce
   Vegetable cooking spray
¼ teaspoon garlic powder
¼ teaspoon ground ginger
4 cups broccoli flowerets
4 cups hot cooked rice

1. Slice beef into very thin strips. In bowl mix cornstarch, *1 cup* broth, sugar and soy until smooth. Set aside.

2. Spray medium skillet with cooking spray and heat over medium-high heat 1 minute. Add beef in 2 batches and stir-fry until browned. Set beef aside.

3. Add remaining broth, garlic powder, ginger and broccoli. Heat to a boil. Reduce heat to low. Cover and cook 5 minutes or until broccoli is tender-crisp.

4. Stir cornstarch mixture and add. Cook until mixture boils and thickens, stirring constantly. Return beef to pan. Heat through. Serve over rice. If desired, garnish with *green onion.*

MAKES 4 SERVINGS • PREP TIME: 15 MINUTES • COOK TIME: 25 MINUTES

✦ *6 grams total fat per serving*

*Think thin—
choose leaner cuts of beef (sirloin, top round
or tenderloin) and trim all visible fat
before slicing or cooking.*

Herb Grilled Chicken

 1 **can (14½ ounces) SWANSON Chicken Broth**
 3 **tablespoons lemon juice**
 1 **teaspoon dried basil leaves, crushed**
 1 **teaspoon dried thyme leaves, crushed**
 ⅛ **teaspoon pepper**
 4 **chicken breast halves (about 2 pounds), skinned**

1. Mix broth, lemon juice, basil, thyme and pepper. Set aside.

2. Place chicken on lightly oiled grill rack over medium-hot coals. Grill uncovered 20 minutes, turning often. Brush with broth mixture and grill 20 minutes more or until chicken is no longer pink, turning and brushing often with broth mixture.

MAKES 4 SERVINGS • PREP TIME: 10 MINUTES • COOK TIME: 40 MINUTES

◆ *4 grams total fat per serving*

VARIATION: Prepare as in Step 1. Place chicken on rack in broiler pan. Broil 6 inches from heat 30 minutes or until chicken is no longer pink, turning and brushing often with broth mixture.

Quick Seasoned Potatoes

 1   **can (14½ ounces) SWANSON Vegetable Broth**
     Generous dash pepper
 1⅓ **cups instant mashed potato flakes *or* buds**

In medium saucepan over medium-high heat, heat broth and pepper to a boil. Remove from heat. Stir in potato flakes until broth is absorbed.

MAKES 4 SERVINGS • PREP TIME: 5 MINUTES • COOK TIME: 5 MINUTES

◆ *Less than 1 gram total fat per serving*

Glazed Pork Chops with Corn Stuffing

1 **can (14½ ounces) SWANSON NATURAL GOODNESS Chicken Broth**
⅛ **teaspoon ground red pepper**
1 **cup frozen whole kernel corn**
1 **stalk celery, chopped (about ½ cup)**
1 **medium onion, chopped (about ½ cup)**
4 **cups PEPPERIDGE FARM Corn Bread Stuffing**
6 **boneless pork chops, ¾ inch thick (about 1½ pounds)**
2 **tablespoons packed brown sugar**
2 **teaspoons spicy-brown mustard**

1. In large saucepan mix broth, pepper, corn, celery and onion. Over medium-high heat, heat to a boil. Remove from heat. Add stuffing. Mix lightly.

2. Spoon into greased 3-quart shallow baking dish. Arrange chops over stuffing. Mix sugar and mustard. Spread over chops.

3. Bake at 400°F. for 30 minutes or until chops are no longer pink.

MAKES 6 SERVINGS • PREP TIME: 20 MINUTES • COOK TIME: 30 MINUTES

✦ *10 grams total fat per serving*

*Prepared mustards are made
of tiny seeds from the mustard plant. The seeds are
white, yellow or black and are first dried, then ground into a paste
with water, vinegar or wine. Generally, the more yellow the
mustard, the milder the taste or pungency.*

Glazed Pork Chops with Corn Stuffing

Garden Vegetable Stuffing

1 can (14½ ounces) SWANSON NATURAL GOODNESS Chicken Broth *or* SWANSON Chicken Broth
3 cups cut-up vegetables*
5 cups PEPPERIDGE FARM Cubed Herb Seasoned Stuffing

1. In large saucepan mix broth and vegetables. Over medium-high heat, heat to a boil. Reduce heat to low. Cover and cook 5 minutes or until vegetables are tender-crisp. Remove from heat. Add stuffing. Mix lightly.

2. Spoon into 1½-quart casserole. Bake at 350°F. for 20 minutes or until hot.

MAKES 8 SERVINGS • PREP TIME: 20 MINUTES • COOK TIME: 20 MINUTES

◆ *2 grams total fat per serving*

* Use a combination of broccoli flowerets, sliced carrot, cauliflower flowerets and sliced celery.

When selecting cauliflower—the "flowered cabbage"— look for a firm, compact head that's creamy white in color. A yellow tint and spreading flowerets with moist brown blotches indicate the cauliflower is past its peak of freshness.

Harvest Fruit Stuffing

  1 **can (14½ ounces) SWANSON Chicken Broth**
  ¼ **cup apple juice**
  1 **cup cut-up mixed dried fruit *or* ½ cup raisins**
  1 **stalk celery, sliced (about ½ cup)**
  1 **medium onion, chopped (about ½ cup)**
  5 **cups PEPPERIDGE FARM Cubed Herb Seasoned Stuffing**

1. In large saucepan mix broth, apple juice, dried fruit, celery and onion. Over medium-high heat, heat to a boil. Reduce heat to low. Cover and cook 5 minutes or until vegetables are tender. Remove from heat. Add stuffing. Mix lightly.

2. Spoon into 1½-quart casserole. Bake at 350°F. for 20 minutes or until hot.

Makes 8 servings • Prep Time: 20 minutes • Cook Time: 20 minutes

✦ *2 grams total fat per serving*

Herbed Vegetable Stuffing

  1 **can (14½ ounces) SWANSON NATURAL GOODNESS Chicken Broth**
      Generous dash pepper
  1 **stalk celery, coarsely chopped (about ½ cup)**
  ½ **cup sliced mushrooms**
  1 **small onion, coarsely chopped (about ¼ cup)**
  4 **cups PEPPERIDGE FARM Herb Seasoned Stuffing**

1. In medium saucepan mix broth, pepper, celery, mushrooms and onion. Over medium-high heat, heat to a boil. Reduce heat to low. Cover and cook 5 minutes or until vegetables are tender. Remove from heat. Add stuffing. Mix lightly.

2. Spoon into 1½-quart casserole. Bake at 350°F. for 20 minutes or until hot.

Makes 8 servings • Prep Time: 15 minutes • Cook Time: 20 minutes

✦ *1 gram total fat per serving*

Harvest Fruit Stuffing

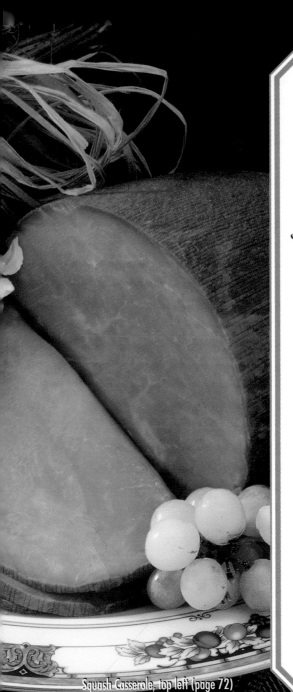

Splendid Sides & Sweets

Side dishes with substance can turn a simple grilled meat and salad into a momentous meal. From traditions with a twist, like *Snappy Macaroni and Cheese*, to a *Vegetable-Dill Stuffing*, these easy-to-prepare recipes bring new zest to everyday meals. And for a sweet ending to a great meal, serve taste-tempting *Cinnamon Bread Pudding* or *Scalloped Apple Bake.*

Squash Casserole, top left (page 72) and Scalloped Apple Bake, bottom left (page 73).

Squash Casserole

3 cups PEPPERIDGE FARM Corn Bread *or* Herb Seasoned Stuffing
¼ cup margarine *or* butter, melted
1 can (10¾ ounces) CAMPBELL'S condensed Cream of Chicken Soup
½ cup sour cream
2 small yellow squash, shredded (about 2 cups)
2 small zucchini, shredded (about 2 cups)
¼ cup shredded carrot
½ cup shredded Cheddar cheese (2 ounces)

1. Mix stuffing and margarine. Reserve *½ cup* stuffing mixture. Spoon remaining stuffing mixture into 2-quart shallow baking dish.

2. Mix soup, sour cream, yellow squash, zucchini, carrot and cheese. Spread over stuffing mixture. Sprinkle reserved stuffing mixture over soup mixture.

3. Bake at 350°F. for 40 minutes or until hot. If desired, garnish with *fresh oregano* and *yellow squash.*

MAKES 8 SERVINGS • PREP TIME: 15 MINUTES • COOK TIME: 40 MINUTES

Whether it's green or yellow, squash is one of the most vividly versatile vegetables! Look for squash with tender, glossy skins free from bruises and blemishes. Choose squash that are slender in diameter and about 6 to 7 inches long.

Scalloped Apple Bake

- ¼ cup margarine *or* butter, melted
- ¼ cup sugar
- 2 teaspoons grated orange peel
- 1 teaspoon ground cinnamon
- 1½ cups PEPPERIDGE FARM Corn Bread Stuffing
- ½ cup coarsely chopped pecans
- 1 can (16 ounces) whole berry cranberry sauce
- ⅓ cup orange juice *or* water
- 4 large cooking apples, cored and thinly sliced (about 6 cups)

1. Lightly mix margarine, sugar, orange peel, cinnamon, stuffing and pecans. Set aside.

2. Mix cranberry sauce, juice and apples. Add *half* stuffing mixture. Mix lightly. Spoon into 8-inch square baking dish. Sprinkle remaining stuffing mixture over apple mixture.

3. Bake at 375°F. for 40 minutes or until apples are tender.

MAKES 6 SERVINGS • PREP TIME: 25 MINUTES • COOK TIME: 40 MINUTES

Sausage Corn Bread Stuffing

- ¼ pound bulk pork sausage
- 1¼ cups water
- 1 tablespoon chopped fresh parsley *or* 1 teaspoon dried parsley flakes
- ½ cup cooked whole kernel corn
- ½ cup shredded Cheddar cheese (2 ounces)
- 4 cups PEPPERIDGE FARM Corn Bread Stuffing

1. In large saucepan over medium-high heat, cook sausage until browned, stirring to separate meat. Pour off fat.

2. Stir in water, parsley, corn and cheese. Add stuffing. Mix lightly. Spoon into greased 1½-quart casserole.

3. Cover and bake at 350°F. for 25 minutes or until hot.

MAKES 6 SERVINGS • PREP TIME: 15 MINUTES • COOK TIME: 25 MINUTES

Golden Pea and Onion Bake

        4 **tablespoons margarine** *or* **butter**
   1½ **cups PEPPERIDGE FARM Corn Bread Stuffing**
        2 **tablespoons chopped fresh parsley**
        3 **large onions, cut in half and sliced (about 3 cups)**
        1 **can (10¾ ounces) CAMPBELL'S condensed Cream of Mushroom Soup**
      ¼ **cup milk**
        1 **cup frozen peas**
        1 **cup shredded Cheddar cheese (4 ounces)**

1. Melt *2 tablespoons* margarine and mix with stuffing and parsley. Set aside.

2. In medium skillet over medium heat, heat remaining margarine. Add onions and cook until tender.

3. Stir in soup, milk and peas. Spoon into 2-quart shallow baking dish. Sprinkle cheese and stuffing mixture over soup mixture.

4. Bake at 350°F. for 30 minutes or until hot.

MAKES 6 SERVINGS • PREP TIME: 15 MINUTES • COOK TIME: 30 MINUTES

Snappy Macaroni and Cheese

        2 **cans (10¾ ounces** *each***) CAMPBELL'S condensed Cheddar Cheese Soup**
   1½ **cups milk**
        2 **tablespoons Dijon-style mustard**
   1½ **cups frozen sugar snap peas**
        1 **medium green** *or* **red pepper, diced (about 1 cup)**
        3 **cups hot cooked elbow macaroni**
      ¼ **cup water**
        2 **tablespoons margarine** *or* **butter, melted**
        4 **cups PEPPERIDGE FARM Corn Bread Stuffing**

1. In 3-quart shallow baking dish mix soup, milk, mustard, snap peas, pepper and macaroni.

2. Mix water and margarine. Add stuffing. Mix lightly. Sprinkle over soup mixture.

3. Bake at 400°F. for 30 minutes or until hot.

MAKES 8 SERVINGS • PREP TIME: 25 MINUTES • COOK TIME: 30 MINUTES

Savory Vegetable Stuffing Bake

  ¼ **pound bulk pork sausage**
  1 **large onion, chopped (about 1 cup)**
  ½ **teaspoon dried thyme leaves, crushed**
  1 **can (10¾ ounces) CAMPBELL'S condensed Cream of Celery Soup**
  1 **can (about 8 ounces) stewed tomatoes**
  2 **cups frozen vegetable combination (broccoli, corn, red pepper)** *or*
      frozen broccoli cuts
  3 **cups PEPPERIDGE FARM Herb Seasoned Stuffing**

1. In large saucepan over medium-high heat, cook sausage, onion and thyme until sausage is browned, stirring to separate meat. Pour off fat.

2. Stir in soup, tomatoes and vegetables. Heat to a boil. Remove from heat. Add stuffing. Mix lightly. Spoon into 1½-quart casserole.

3. Bake at 350°F. for 30 minutes or until hot.

MAKES 6 SERVINGS • PREP TIME: 20 MINUTES • COOK TIME: 30 MINUTES

Stuffing Florentine

  4 **cups PEPPERIDGE FARM Herb Seasoned Stuffing**
  1 **tablespoon margarine** *or* **butter, melted**
  1 **can (10¾ ounces) CAMPBELL'S condensed Cream of Celery Soup**
  ½ **cup sour cream**
  1 **teaspoon onion powder**
  1 **package (about 10 ounces) frozen chopped spinach, thawed**
  ¼ **cup grated Parmesan cheese**

1. Mix ½ *cup* stuffing and margarine. Set aside.

2. Mix soup, sour cream, onion powder, spinach and cheese. Add remaining stuffing. Mix lightly. Spoon into 1½-quart casserole. Sprinkle reserved stuffing mixture over soup mixture.

3. Bake at 350°F. for 35 minutes or until hot.

MAKES 6 SERVINGS • PREP TIME: 10 MINUTES • COOK TIME: 35 MINUTES

Savory Vegetable Stuffing Bake

Parslied Potato Stuffing

  ¼ **cup margarine _or_ butter**
  2 **stalks celery, chopped (about 1 cup)**
  1 **large onion, chopped (about 1 cup)**
  ¼ **teaspoon pepper**
  1 **can (14½ ounces) SWANSON Chicken Broth**
  ¼ **cup chopped fresh parsley**
  3 **cups cubed cooked potatoes (about 3 medium)**
  4 **cups PEPPERIDGE FARM Cubed Herb Seasoned Stuffing**

1. In large saucepan over medium heat, heat margarine. Add celery, onion and pepper and cook until tender.

2. Stir in broth and parsley. Add potatoes and stuffing. Mix lightly. Spoon into 2-quart casserole.

3. Bake at 350°F. for 25 minutes or until hot.

MAKES 8 SERVINGS • PREP TIME: 25 MINUTES • COOK TIME: 25 MINUTES

Vegetable-Dill Stuffing

  ¼ **cup margarine _or_ butter**
  2 **stalks celery, chopped (about 1 cup)**
  2 **tablespoons chopped onion**
  1 **can (14½ ounces) SWANSON Vegetable Broth**
  4 **cups PEPPERIDGE FARM Herb Seasoned Stuffing**
  ⅓ **cup VLASIC Dill Relish**

1. In large saucepan over medium heat, heat margarine. Add celery and onion and cook until tender.

2. Add broth. Heat to a boil. Remove from heat. Add stuffing and relish. Mix lightly. Cover and let stand 5 minutes.

MAKES 6 SERVINGS • PREP TIME: 10 MINUTES • COOK TIME: 10 MINUTES • STAND TIME: 5 MINUTES

Parslied Potato Stuffing

Cinnamon Bread Pudding

  6 cups cubed PEPPERIDGE FARM Cinnamon Swirl Bread
  ½ cup raisins
  4 eggs, beaten
2½ cups milk
  ½ cup sugar
  1 teaspoon vanilla extract
  Sweetened whipped cream (optional)

1. Place bread in greased 2-quart shallow baking dish. Sprinkle raisins over bread. Mix eggs, milk, sugar and vanilla. Pour over bread.

2. Bake at 350°F. for 40 minutes or until knife inserted near center comes out clean. Serve warm with whipped cream. If desired, garnish with *cinnamon stick, mint leaf* and *confectioners' sugar*.

MAKES 6 SERVINGS • PREP TIME: 15 MINUTES • COOK TIME: 40 MINUTES

An easy make-ahead dessert or brunch item, this bread pudding can be prepared the day before. Simply cover and refrigerate up to 24 hours before baking!

Any-Occasion Appetizers

*E*ntertaining is easy when you rely on this assortment of simple snacks and appetizers. Versatile recipes, like *Salsa Onion Dip* and *Crunchy Chicken Nibbles,* shine at casual get-togethers and dressy holiday affairs. Hearty hot appetizers, like *Savory Stuffed Mushrooms* and *Chicken "Cheese Steak" Sandwiches,* give munchers a memorable feast.

Pictured clockwise from left: Fiesta Nachos (page 84), Mozzarella Cheese
Bread Sticks (page 85) and Savory Stuffed Mushrooms (page 85`

Fiesta Nachos

>   1   can (11 ounces) CAMPBELL'S condensed Fiesta Nacho Cheese Soup
>   ⅓   cup water
>   1   bag (about 10 ounces) tortilla chips
>   Chopped tomato
>   Sliced green onions
>   Sliced VLASIC *or* EARLY CALIFORNIA pitted Ripe Olives
>   Chopped green *and/or* red pepper

1. In small saucepan mix soup and water. Over low heat, heat through, stirring often.

2. Serve over tortilla chips. Top with tomato, onions, olives and pepper. If desired, garnish with *green onion.*

MAKES 6 SERVINGS • PREP TIME: 10 MINUTES • COOK TIME: 5 MINUTES

Chicken "Cheese Steak" Sandwiches

>   1   loaf (11¾ ounces) PEPPERIDGE FARM frozen Monterey Jack and
>   Jalapeño Cheese Bread
>   ½   pound skinless, boneless chicken breasts, cut into strips
>   ⅛   teaspoon garlic powder
>   3   teaspoons vegetable oil
>   1   small green *and/or* red pepper, cut into 2-inch-long strips (about 1 cup)
>   1   medium onion, sliced (about ½ cup)

1. Preheat oven to 350°F. Cut bread bag at one end. Place on baking sheet in center of oven. Bake 25 minutes or until hot.

2. Sprinkle chicken with garlic powder. In medium skillet over medium-high heat, heat *2 teaspoons* oil. Add chicken and cook until browned, stirring often. Set chicken aside.

3. Reduce heat to medium. Add remaining oil. Add pepper and onion and cook until tender. Return chicken to pan and heat through.

4. Remove bread from bag. Separate bread halves. Spoon chicken mixture on bottom bread half and top with remaining bread half. Cut into quarters or 1-inch slices.

MAKES 4 SANDWICHES OR 12 APPETIZERS • PREP TIME: 10 MINUTES • COOK TIME: 25 MINUTES

Savory Stuffed Mushrooms

24 medium mushrooms (about 1 pound)
 6 tablespoons margarine *or* butter
 1 small onion, chopped (about ¼ cup)
 ¼ teaspoon garlic powder *or* 2 cloves garlic, minced
 1 package (3 ounces) cream cheese, softened
 3 tablespoons grated Parmesan cheese
 2 tablespoons chopped fresh parsley *or* 2 teaspoons dried parsley flakes
 1 cup PEPPERIDGE FARM Herb Seasoned Stuffing

1. Remove stems from mushrooms. Chop enough stems to make *1 cup* and set aside.

2. In medium saucepan over medium heat, melt *2 tablespoons* margarine. Brush mushroom caps with margarine and place top-side down in shallow baking pan. In same saucepan heat remaining margarine. Add chopped mushroom stems, onion and garlic powder and cook until tender.

3. Stir in cream cheese, Parmesan cheese and parsley. Add stuffing. Mix lightly. Spoon about *1 tablespoon* stuffing mixture into each mushroom cap.

4. Bake at 425°F. for 10 minutes or until mushrooms are heated through. If desired, garnish with *fresh chervil*.

MAKES 24 APPETIZERS • PREP TIME: 25 MINUTES • COOK TIME: 10 MINUTES

Mozzarella Cheese Bread Sticks

1 loaf (11¾ ounces) PEPPERIDGE FARM frozen Mozzarella
     Garlic Cheese Bread
 1½ cups PREGO Traditional Spaghetti Sauce

1. Preheat oven to 350°F. Cut bread bag at one end and place on baking sheet in center of oven. Bake 25 minutes or until hot.

2. Remove bread from bag. Cut each bread half into 12 slices.

3. Pour spaghetti sauce into microwave-safe bowl. Cover and microwave on HIGH 2 minutes or until hot. Serve with bread for dipping.

MAKES 24 APPETIZERS • PREP TIME: 10 MINUTES • COOK TIME: 25 MINUTES

Crunchy Chicken Nibbles

1½ pounds skinless, boneless chicken breasts, cut into 1-inch pieces
1 jar (12 ounces) refrigerated MARIE'S Honey Mustard Dressing and Dip
2 cups PEPPERIDGE FARM Herb Seasoned Stuffing, crushed
2 tablespoons orange juice

1. Dip chicken into *¾ cup* dressing. Coat with stuffing.

2. Place chicken on baking sheet. Bake at 400°F. for 15 minutes or until chicken is no longer pink.

3. In small saucepan mix remaining dressing and orange juice. Over medium heat, heat through. Serve with chicken for dipping.

MAKES ABOUT 40 APPETIZERS • PREP TIME: 15 MINUTES • COOK TIME: 15 MINUTES

Mushroom Stuffing Balls

½ cup margarine *or* butter, melted
4 eggs, beaten
2 tablespoons chopped fresh parsley *or* 2 teaspoons dried parsley flakes
⅛ teaspoon garlic powder *or* 1 clove garlic, minced
2½ cups chopped mushrooms (about 8 ounces)
1 medium onion, chopped (about ½ cup)
½ cup grated Parmesan cheese
2½ cups PEPPERIDGE FARM Herb Seasoned Stuffing

1. Mix margarine, eggs, parsley, garlic powder, mushrooms, onion and cheese. Add stuffing. Mix lightly. Shape into 32 (1-inch) balls and place 2 inches apart on baking sheets.

2. Bake at 350°F. for 15 minutes or until golden.

MAKES 32 APPETIZERS • PREP TIME: 25 MINUTES • COOK TIME: 15 MINUTES

TIP: To make ahead, shape into balls and place on baking sheet. Freeze. When frozen, store in plastic bag up to one month. To bake, place frozen balls on baking sheets and bake at 350°F. for 20 minutes or until golden.

Crunchy Chicken Nibbles

Salsa Onion Dip

    1 **pouch CAMPBELL'S Dry Onion Soup and Recipe Mix**
    1 **container (16 ounces) sour cream**
    1 **cup PACE Thick & Chunky Salsa**
       Assorted fresh vegetables *or* chips

Mix soup mix, sour cream and salsa. Refrigerate at least 2 hours. Serve with fresh vegetables or chips for dipping. If desired, garnish with *green onion.*

MAKES 3 CUPS • PREP TIME: 5 MINUTES • CHILL TIME: 2 HOURS

Stuffed Clams

  24 **cherrystone clams, scrubbed**
    2 **slices bacon, diced**
    3 **tablespoons margarine *or* butter**
    1 **medium onion, chopped (about $\frac{1}{2}$ cup)**
  $\frac{1}{4}$ **teaspoon garlic powder *or* 2 cloves garlic, minced**
$1\frac{1}{2}$ **cups PEPPERIDGE FARM Herb Seasoned Stuffing**
    2 **tablespoons grated Parmesan cheese**
    2 **tablespoons chopped fresh parsley *or* 2 teaspoons dried parsley flakes**

1. Open clams. Remove and discard top shell. Arrange clams in large shallow baking pan.

2. In medium skillet over medium heat, cook bacon until crisp. Remove and drain on paper towels.

3. Add margarine, onion and garlic powder to hot drippings. Cook until tender. Add stuffing, cheese, parsley and bacon. Mix lightly. Spoon on top of each clam.

4. Bake at 400°F. for 20 minutes or until done.

MAKES 24 APPETIZERS • PREP TIME: 35 MINUTES • COOK TIME: 20 MINUTES

Cheddar Vegetable Melt Sandwiches

1 loaf (11¾ ounces) PEPPERIDGE FARM frozen Two Cheddar Cheese Bread
1 cup water
2 cups fresh *or* frozen broccoli flowerets
2 teaspoons vegetable oil
1 cup sliced mushrooms (about 3 ounces)
⅛ teaspoon garlic powder
1 medium tomato, sliced

1. Preheat oven to 350°F. Cut bread bag at one end. Place on baking sheet in center of oven. Bake 25 minutes or until hot.

2. In medium saucepan mix water and broccoli. Over high heat, heat to a boil. Reduce heat to low. Cover and cook 5 minutes or until broccoli is tender-crisp. Drain in colander.

3. In same saucepan over medium heat, heat oil. Add mushrooms and garlic powder and cook until tender. Return broccoli to pan and heat through.

4. Remove bread from bag. Separate bread halves. Arrange tomato slices on bottom bread half. Top with broccoli mixture and remaining bread half. Cut into quarters or 1-inch slices.

MAKES 4 SANDWICHES OR 12 APPETIZERS • PREP TIME: 10 MINUTES • COOK TIME: 25 MINUTES

Selecting the freshest mushrooms is a beauty contest, so choose only the most attractive. The caps should be firm, bright and bruise-free. The gills underneath the cap should be tightly closed.

Cheddar Vegetable Melt Sandwiches (top)
Chicken "Cheese Steak" Sandwiches (bottom, recipe page 84).

Recipes By Product Index

Recipes By Product Index (continued)

Recipe Index

Recipe Index (continued)

BETTER THAN A BREAD CRUMB! STUFFING TIPS

Pepperidge Farm bakes the finest blend of herbs and spices into *all* their special stuffing breads. In addition to stuffing poultry, use stuffing, the perfectly seasoned ingredient with lots of baked-in flavor, for a variety of family-pleasing casseroles (see *Casseroles on the Quick,* page 4). Or, for extra flavor and texture, stuffing makes a tasty, crispy coating for chicken, pork or fish (see *Sensational Suppers in a Snap,* page 32). With the varieties and versatility of PEPPERIDGE FARM Stuffings, it's easy to see that stuffing is *Better than a Bread Crumb!*

Here's a handy reference chart to help you measure how much stuffing you'll need to prepare for roast turkey or chicken. Follow the easy preparation instructions on the package and use the amounts in the chart below to make stuffing as a side dish for chicken, pork chops or fish.

Poultry Uncooked	PEPPERIDGE FARM Stuffing	Water*	Margarine or Butter	Number of People Served**
14-16 lb. Turkey	16 oz. pkg.	2½ cups	8 tbsp.	about 11
5-9 lb. Poultry	6 cups	2 cups	6 tbsp.	8
4 Boneless Chicken Breasts	3 cups	1 cup	3 tbsp.	4
2 Boneless Chicken Breasts	1½ cups	½ cup	1 1/2 tbsp.	2

* For more moist stuffing, increase water by 2-4 tablespoons per 16-ounce package.
** Based on ¾ cup serving size.

Stuffing Tips:
• For a more delicious flavor, substitute **SWANSON** Broth for water.
• To add your own personal touch, add one or any combination of the following, up to 3 cups per 16-ounce package:

1 cup sautéed chopped celery	1 cup sautéed chopped onion
2 cups sautéed mushrooms	1 cup chopped walnuts, pecans or cooked chestnuts
Chopped, cooked giblets	1 cup cooked and drained sausage
2 cups chopped cranberries	

Turkey Tips:
Just follow these directions below to help make your next turkey dinner with all the trimmings a savory success!
• Allow about ½ cup stuffing per pound of turkey or just enough stuffing to fill the turkey.
• Pack stuffing lightly in the turkey to allow room for expansion.
• Stuff the turkey just before roasting, *never ahead of time.*
• Extra stuffing may be baked separately in a covered casserole dish for the last 30 minutes of roasting time.
• After turkey is done, check the stuffing temperature with a meat thermometer. Fully cooked stuffing should reach 165°F.
• Remove stuffing from turkey *immediately* after dinner.
• The U.S. Department of Agriculture operates a toll-free Meat & Poultry Hotline. The nationwide number is 1 (800) 535-4555. Home economists will answer meat and poultry questions Monday through Friday, 10:00 a.m. to 4:00 p.m., EST.
• Remember, PEPPERIDGE FARM Gravy makes the perfect accompaniment to your turkey and stuffing (see recipe, page 52).